*I*ntroduction

Rubber stamping, which was once considered kids' play, has become one of the most exciting means of creating artistic designs for cards, packages, T-shirts, and more. Because rubber stamping is so quick, easy and fun, it has become the hobby of the 90's. Once you begin rubber stamping, you will be amazed with the many ways stamps can be used and the instant success you can achieve by simply adding color to your stamps.

This book includes:
- **The basics of rubber stamping**
- **Supplies available**
- **Illustrated instructions**
- **Full color examples on each page**
- **Pages and pages of stamping ideas**
- **Special stamping tips at the bottom of each page**
- **A glossary of common rubber stamp terms and supplies**

A Special Thank-you to the Stamp Companies and people who helped make this book possible:

A Stamp-In-The-Hand
Commotion
Printworks
Stampendous
Wangs
Kat Okamoto
Kevin Nakagawa
Vicki Shirley
Francis Orlando
Jim Koch Studio
Joseph Angeli

Printed in Hong Kong

CAUTION: Rubber stamping is habit forming!

Table of Contents

Basic Supplies

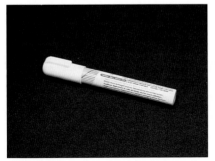

Stamps. It is best to begin with two to three word stamps ("Thank You," "Happy Birthday," etc.) and three to five picture stamps. Try to choose subject matter that you are interested in such as sea shells, flowers, etc.

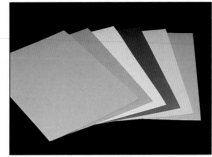

Papers. Stamp on plastic coated (gloss) paper for a bold and dramatic effect. Use non-gloss paper when you want a more subtle image.

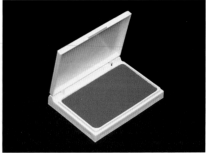

Solid Color Stamp Pad. Stamp pads come in a wide variety of colors. Choose two or three different colors if you are just beginning. There are also **Rainbow Stamp Pads** that have two or more colors in them.

Colored Markers. A set of water based colored markers will allow you to color directly on your rubber stamp for a variety of visual images.

Glitter Glue. This is glue mixed with colored or clear glitter. It comes in a small squeezable container and takes 2-4 hours to dry. This glitter is fun to use and adds a sparkle to brighten up your design. It's also great for disguising little mistakes.

Dry Glitter. This glitter comes in a shaker top bottle in a variety of colors. Use a *fine* or *sand* coarseness. This will add a hint of color without overpowering your stamped images.

Glue Stick. Conveniently in pen form, this glue can be used to add dry glitter, embossing powder, and decorations.

Pigment Ink Pads. These are slow drying ink pads which are used primarily for embossing. They come in both solid (one color) and multi-color.

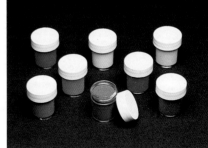

Embossing Powder. This powder, combined with a slow drying ink (pigment) pad and heat gives your work a sophisticated, raised look. Powders are available in many colors, including neon.

TIP... Refrigerating your stamp pads will give them a longer life and keep your rainbow pad colors more clear and defined.

   4

Stamp $C$are and Storage

There are a number of commercial stamp cleaners that work well, but you can easily clean your stamps using a mixture of one part glass cleaner to four parts water. Clean your stamps after each stamping to minimize ink build-up which can reduce the sharpness of your image. **To clean stamps:** Stack five paper towels on a cookie sheet, spray generously with cleaning solution and stamp on the moist towels until the ink is removed. Follow these basic rules for years of trouble-free stamping.

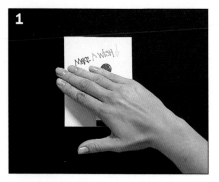

1. Stamp

2. Clean

3. Store

Rubber stamp clean-up pads are available to replace paper towels. The procedure for cleaning your stamps with a stamp pad is the same as the paper towel method. When you are finished, the pad is easily cleaned by rinsing with water and standing it on end to dry.

You may find you have ink on your fingers after stamping. Soap and water will not remove the ink and household cleaners are harsh on your hands. Hand cleaner bars are made just for cleaning hands. They last and last and work like no other cleaner to remove ink stains. Wet the bar and rub on hands where you have ink and in seconds the stains are gone! Hand cleaner bars are available at stamp stores and some craft stores.

Storage

The best way to store stamps is in lucite picture frames which come in a variety of sizes. Use small ones to separate by subject or use a large frame to store all of your stamps. This also makes them easily stackable and portable. To make storage easy, stamp all of your rubber stamps on a piece of paper that fits inside the lucite frame. Then you can quickly locate and replace your stamps back in the same spot each time.

TIP... Store stamps by subject matter (i.e. word stamps, flower stamps, etc.) and leave space around each subject for additional stamps.

Let's Get Started

Now that we've covered basic supplies, stamp care, and storage, let's start stamping! For those of you who have never stamped before, begin with a word stamp and one to three decorative stamps for your card. Let's begin by making a card using a stamp pad and then we'll try coloring, glitter, and more....

Stamping with a Stamp Pad

- **Press stamp into ink pad gently, being careful not to press or rock your stamp too hard or you'll get ink on the outer wooden edge of your stamp. For larger stamps, apply more pressure.**
- **Set stamp in place on your card.**
- **Press firmly and evenly with the palm of your hand.**

Coloring Directly on Rubber Stamp with Water-based Markers

By coloring your stamps as you would a coloring book, you can create more interest and excitement. You can color the same stamp in a variety of color combinations and create a different effect with each stamping.

- **Color the stamp beginning with your lightest color first to keep light colors light. Hold pen at 45 degree angle so just the top surface of the stamp is colored.**
- **Set stamp in place on your card.**

Coloring on Card after Stamping

When you have stamps that are outlines, you can color the stamp after stamping it on your card.

- **Ink your rubber stamp with either a stamp pad or a marker.**
- **Stamp your image.**
- **Then color it in with markers.**

TIP... After coloring a stamp with markers, moisten the stamp by exhaling one long slow breath. This will help to restore any color which may have dried.

Adding Glitter

You can use dry glitter which is easy to apply and dries in five minutes or use glitter glue and simply squeeze it onto the desired area. It will dry in 2-4 hours with brilliant color.

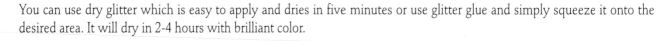

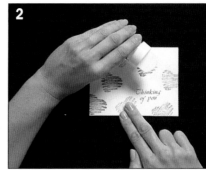

Using Dry Glitter and a Glue Stick

1. Stamp your card using ink pads or markers. Apply glue stick to areas where you want glitter. Remember, your inks are water based, so just accent. If you try to color with the glue stick, your ink will run.

2. Shake glitter *(fine or sand thickness works best)* onto glued area. Tap off excess into folded card and pour back into glitter jar.

Using Glitter Glue

- **Stamp your card using ink pads or markers.**
- **Apply glitter glue to areas you want to highlight.**
- **Allow glue to dry 2-4 hours. As the glitter glue dries, the color will become bolder.**

TIP... When stamping, remember that odd numbers look better. For example, use a cluster of three or five ballons instead of two or four. Put three different stamps on a card instead of two or four, etc.

Repeating Patterns

One stamp can go a long way when it is used to make patterns, borders or clusters. Stamp across the bottom, up the sides, or all around the card with the same rubber stamp to create a pattern or border. Borders can be stamped straight or tilted. Alternate the angle of your stamp when doing a border. This way, you don't have to be concerned about it being perfectly straight or even.

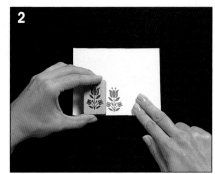

Making a Centered Border

1. Ink stamp with stamp pads or markers. Center the first stamped image on the bottom of your card by measuring either by eye or with a ruler for the center point of the card. Stamp image.

2. Re-ink with same colors or clean and use different colors for the adjacent stamp. Line up your second stamp with the edge of your centered stamped image. Repeat step two until complete. **Note:** You may need to make adjustments if your stamp is mounted crooked or off center, but with good quality stamps this is generally not a problem.

Creating Distance

1. Stamp images toward the bottom of your page, re-inking with each stamping.

2. Without re-inking, stamp more images higher up on the card, overlap-ping the lower row or grouping and varying the heights.

TIP... To show movement such as a bird flying; stamp a dark image of the stamp, then stamp away from the bird and the image will get lighter and lighter.

Sponging *and* Stenciling

Use a sponge to create beautiful frames, borders, backgrounds, and a number of special effects. Different sponges will give different effects depending on the texture and content. For a soft look use cosmetic sponges. For a more sponge-like look, a household sponge works well. Sea sponges give your work a lacy look. You can also purchase small pre-cut sponges and use them to complement and enhance your rubber stamping.

Sponging a Frame

1. Cut sponge to a manageable size. Dab sponge on ink pad or color with marker. Dab lightly on paper towel to remove excess ink.

2. Dab around paper, firmer around the edge and lighter toward the inside to create depth.

To create a frame of color, cover part of your card with a plain piece of paper or doily and stamp or sponge around the mask, keeping an area of your card empty. Use a thin piece of paper for a clean edge and a doily for a lacy look.

Sponging, Using a Stencil or Mask

• **Using a thin piece of paper or a doily, cut out your desired shape and place it on top of the card.**

• **Holding firmly, Stamp or sponge on the card, being sure to overlap onto mask so that the stenciled image will appear when removed. Remove stencil, and add decorations.**

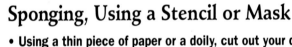

Making a Reverse Stencil

Instead of making a shape to cover an area of your card, you can do the reverse by cutting a shape out of a piece of paper and stamping or sponging inside the shape to create the actual shape instead of a border. Using a thin piece of paper, slightly larger than the card, cut out desired shape and place over card. Stamp or sponge the card, being sure that the inside of the design is stamped or sponged over the edge of the stencil so the image will appear when removed. Remove the stencil and add decorations.

TIP... Cut out a heart shape using a thin piece of paper. Place heart on card and stamp around it using different kinds of heart stamps, remove and you have a heart shape in the middle where you can add a message, a satin ribbon, another stamp etc.

Precious memories,
warm moments with
those you love and
wishes for many
more to come.

Your
kindness
touches
me...

Congratulations

Embossing

Embossing is one of the most exciting techniques to use with stamping! Add embossing powder to an opaque ink stamped image and heat to create elegant cards. You can emboss on most card stocks, construction paper, tissue paper, wood, cardboard, paper napkins, clothing and more! Embossing pens are also available. These slow drying ink pens combined with embossing powder will give your hand written messages and pen drawn designs a raised and shiny look.

Powders and Inks

To emboss, use an opaque pigment ink pad. It's slow drying and will "catch" the embossing powder. There are solid, multi, and clear pigment ink pads along with many colors of powders. The most important thing to remember is that the color of the powder is the color you will get when you emboss. For example, if you use gold ink and silver embossing powder, your image will be primarily silver with some spots of gold. Clear embossing powders will give a clear raised look to whatever color you stamp. "Clear Glitter" powder will raise and add a touch of glitter to your embossed image. Heat activates and melts the powder.

Heating Elements for Embossing

There are a number of heating elements that work well for embossing. A professional heat gun (at low setting) or a craft heat gun is the easiest way to go. These heat controlled devices give steady direct heat. A household iron set on low can also be used by slowly moving the image in a circular motion, face up over the iron. You can also use an electric burner but make sure it is set on low so your paper or fabric doesn't burn. Standard blow driers are not hot enough for this process.

Embosing with Colored Ink and Embossing Powder

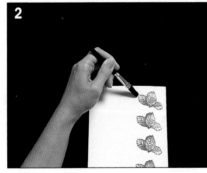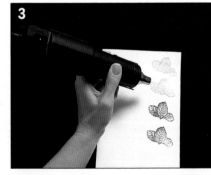

1. Ink with an opaque pigment ink pad and stamp. Pour embossing powder generously over the stamped image. Tap off excess powder and funnel back into jar.

2. Using a clean, dry paint brush, dust excess powder off card.

3. Hold card face up above heating element (when using a heat gun heat directly onto card) and move in a circular motion to keep paper from getting too hot. Embossing powder will rise and become shiny when done.

TIP... You can also emboss with a glue pen.

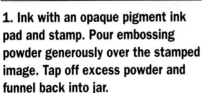

Congratulations

Precious memories,
warm moments with
those you love and
wishes for many
more to come

Here Are Some More Stamping Ideas!

GABRIELLE'S NOTEBOOK

Handmade by

YOU'RE INVITED

LAUREN

BE MY VALENTINE

Positioning

The positioner is one of the most exciting and innovative tools in rubber stamping. This lucite T-square does three things; it enables you to correct your mistakes, put your rubber stamp in the exact location desired, and make straight borders. The T-square has non-slip pads and grid lines for more accurate measuring. Each see-thru paper pad has step by step instructions on the back for use with the positioner. Both of these items are available at rubber stamp stores and some craft stores.

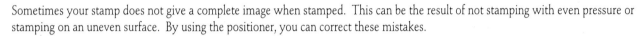

Sometimes your stamp does not give a complete image when stamped. This can be the result of not stamping with even pressure or stamping on an uneven surface. By using the positioner, you can correct these mistakes.

Correcting your Mistakes

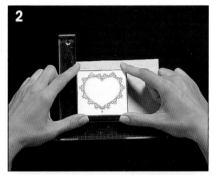

1. Place a sheet of see-thru paper in the "L" of your positioner.

2. Stamp your image on the see-thru paper by guiding the wood block of the stamp firmly into the corner of your positioner.

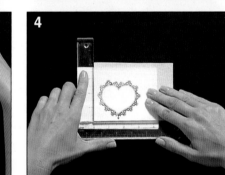

3. Move the see-thru paper image to the spot where you want the image to appear on your card.

4. Hold the see-thru paper securely and place the positioner back to the corner of the paper. Remove the see-thru paper without moving your positioner.

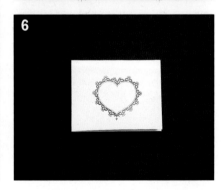

5. Guide your inked stamp into the corner and stamp on your card.

6. Your mistake is now corrected!

TIP... You can use all four corners of each piece of see-thru paper. Keep all stamped papers in an envelope for future use.

    18

Positioning

Hearts, frames and other enclosed borders look nice with a message stamped inside, such as "Thank You" or "Happy Birthday", etc. To nestle a stamp within a frame, follow the steps below.

 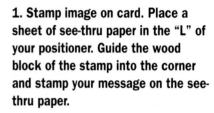 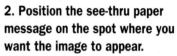 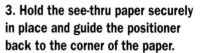

Placing a Stamp in a Specific Spot

1. Stamp image on card. Place a sheet of see-thru paper in the "L" of your positioner. Guide the wood block of the stamp into the corner and stamp your message on the see-thru paper.

2. Position the see-thru paper message on the spot where you want the image to appear.

3. Hold the see-thru paper securely in place and guide the positioner back to the corner of the paper.

4. Remove the see-thru paper without moving your positioner and guide your inked stamp into the corner of the positioner and stamp on your card.

Borders can add a nice finishing touch to your card, but making a straight border can be difficult. By using the method below, you can put every stamp in your border in the exact spot that you want. To make things even simpler, you can use the long side of your positioner to guide your stamp along the edge to create an even border.

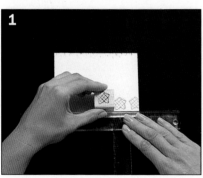 

Making a Straight Border

1. Place the long side of the positioner below the desired border location. Stamp the first image on one side of the edge of your page.

2. Using the wooden edge of your stamp, line up the side of your stamped image with the wooden edge, placing the bottom edge of the wood against the top of the positioner and stamp. Repeat until complete.

TIP... To keep the tissue paper from sliding under the positioner, first lay a piece of card stock under the positioner.

Masking

This simple technique will create the illusion of one image appearing behind the other. By covering an image which has already been stamped, you can stamp over that image without the images overlapping.

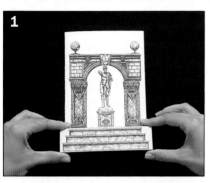
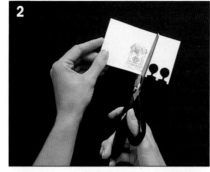

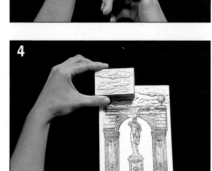

Using Masks

1. Stamp the closest images on the card first. Stamp the same images again on a sticky note, making sure that part of the stamped image is on the sticky edge of the paper.

2. Cut out the image.

3. Place the cut out directly on top of the stamped image to cover it up.

4. Stamp around, and on the mask. When finished, remove the mask.

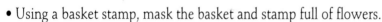

Ideas for Masking

- Using a basket stamp, mask the basket and stamp full of flowers.
- Stamp an animal, cover the mask and surround with trees, flowers, etc.
- Using a frame stamp, cover with mask and fill in with a scene to create the look of a framed picture.
- Cut out a heart shaped "mask", place on card, stamp all around edges and remove mask. Use marker to make a dot outline of the heart. Stamp message in heart *(see Positioning)*.

TIP... To keep images from floating, "ground" them by masking and stamping grass and flowers around the base of your image.

20

Layering

By layering a number of different stamps on top of each other, you can create depth and dimension. An example of this is clustering dried flower stamps to create an upside down bouquet.

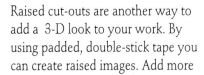
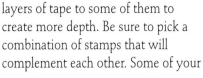

Layering Images

1. Stamp your first image beginning with your lightest color.

2. Repeat stamping, overlapping your images. Add a cut out bow stamp or glue on a ribbon to finish your bouquet.

Raised cut-outs are another way to add a 3-D look to your work. By using padded, double-stick tape you can create raised images. Add more layers of tape to some of them to create more depth. Be sure to pick a combination of stamps that will complement each other. Some of your raised cut-outs should be the same as those stamped on your card to tie the idea together.

Making Raised Cut-Outs

1. Stamp your card with chosen stamps. Stamp complementary images on a second piece of card stock.

2. Cut out images and arrange on card. For creativity, glue some of the cut-outs hanging over the edges of the card. Affix to card using double sided tape. If necessary, trim cut-outs hanging over edges of card.

TIP... Save extra cut-outs in envelopes by subject and use them for last minute decoration of packages, gift tags, cards. You can also use them to cover mistakes.

Die-Cuts

Die-cut cards are cards cut in a particular shape such as a teddy bear, a star, heart, etc. These cards can be bought in pre-cut patterns or made individually by tracing a pattern. Stamping on these cards gives you a whole new look. Try using die-cuts for a party invitation that will really impress your guests.

Using Store Bought Patterns

• **Simply cut out your design and trace it onto card stock.**

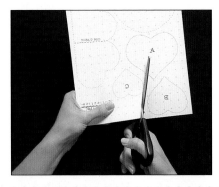

Making your Own Cut-Outs

By using your imagination, you can find items around your house to trace. One example is a paintbrush for a paint party invitaion.

1. **Trace shape on card stock and cut it out.**

2. **Decorate with stamps.** *(see Sponging and Stenciling)*

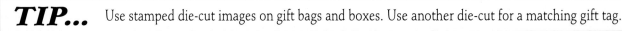

TIP... Use stamped die-cut images on gift bags and boxes. Use another die-cut for a matching gift tag.

YOUR
BIRTHDAY
IS A
CELEBRATION
OF YOU!

Pop-Up Cards

These cards create a 3-D effect when opened. By gluing stamped cut-outs to the "pop-up" area of the card, you can create all kinds of pop-up masterpieces. Blank pop-up cards can be purchased or you can cut, fold and glue your own. These cards are easy to make and much less expensive than purchasing them ready made.

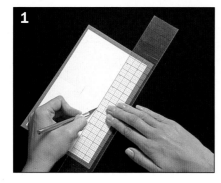
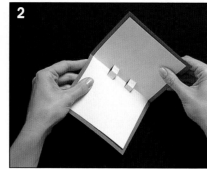

Making Blank Pop-Up Cards that will Fit a Standard 4-1/2" x 5-3/4" Envelope

1. Cut a piece of colored construction paper to 8-1/2" x 5-1/2" (8-1/2" x 11" cut in half). Cut a piece of white construc-tion paper to 8" x 5". With an exacto knife, add four slits where indicated.

2. Fold slit card in half so that you have two sets of slits and fold inward. Glue inside card to ouside card with a glue stick. Be careful not to glue the slit area down. If necessary, trim cut-outs hanging over edges of card.

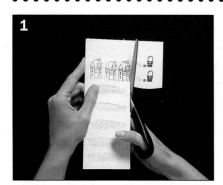
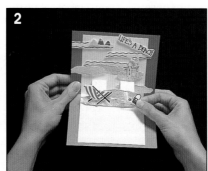

Creating a Pop-Up Card

1. Stamp your images on the card stock of your choice. Cut out all your images and arrange them different ways until you have the look you want.

2. Using double sided tape, attach images to the inverted slits of your card 1/8" above the base to allow for closing.

TIP... For added dimension, add two layers of double sided tape to some of your pop-up card images.

YOU ARE INVITED

SURPRISE
PARTY FOR SUE
SAT. THE 25th
KIM'S HOUSE

·HAPPY·
BIRTHDAY

LIFE'S A BEACH

Fabric Stamping

There are now special ink pads available that turn your stamped images into instant iron-on transfers! Stamp your images onto any paper using the special "Stamp 'N' Iron" ink pads and iron onto your clothing. This is great for anyone who may be reluctant to stamp directly onto fabric. If the design doesn't look good to you on paper, you haven't ruined a shirt. There is no time limit for ironing on fabric once you have stamped your design on paper. You can use your iron-on next month or next year. This process will work best on 50/50 blends. Decorate napkins, placemats, tablecloths, etc. These inks are non-toxic and will not harm the environment. They are water soluable and clean up easily with warm water.

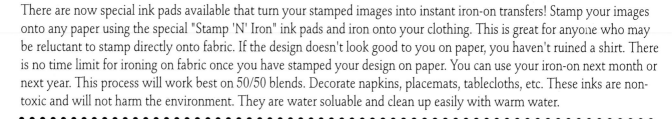

Stamp your designs onto any kind of paper. Thin, semi-translucent paper works well because you can see the design when positioning it on the fabric. Transfer inks, once transfered, will be brighter than the color of the stamped image. The design will also reverse when transfered to the fabric.

Making Fabric Iron-Ons

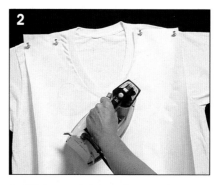

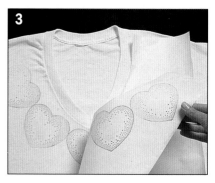

1. Lay fabric on a clean, flat surface such as a table or an ironing board. Place the design, stamped side down, on the fabric and pin it down to make sure it will not shift when ironing.

2. With your iron setting on high (no steam) and with firm and even pressure, slowly iron in one direction and then the opposite direction.

3. Lift one corner of the paper to make sure the image has been transfered. Remove paper and decorate with fabric glitter, bows, etc. You can wear your design immediately but wait 24 hours before washing.

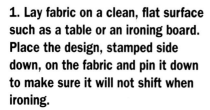

> **TIP...** Send a stamped card to a friend using "Stamp 'N' Iron" ink. Your hand stamped creation can be ironed on a shirt, napkin, apron or any fabric.

Glossary

 Brush Markers. Water-based markers with long, broad tips for coloring in stamped images. They may also be used to color directly on the rubber stamp to give a multi-colored image.

 Cut-Outs. The result of stamping an image, cutting it out and affixing it to card stock with double sided tape to create dimension.

 **Die-Cuts.** Cards pre-cut into shapes such as bears or hearts. They may be decorated alone or layered on a card.

 Double Sided Tape. Tape that is sticky on both sides. Some tape may have a thick layer of foam within itself.

Dry Glitter. Glitter that comes in dry form, in a shaker top jar.

 Embossing. This process gives a raised, shiny finish to your stamped design.

Embossing Ink. A slow drying ink that allows embossing powder to adhere to it.

 Embossing Powder. Powder that is sprinkled on an opaque ink stamped image and heated to create a raised, shiny texture. It comes in a variety of colors including metallics and neons

Fade-Outs. Stamping, without re-inking your stamp causes your image to *fade-out*. This process is great for showing distance or movement.

 Glitter Glue. Glue that has glitter in it and dries clear.

Glue Pen. Looks like a chisel point marking pen. It is used to glue dry glitter to card stock. It can also be used for embossing.

 Heat 'N' Iron Ink Pads. This ink, when applied to any kind of paper, becomes an iron-on transfer. It can then be transfered to fabric.

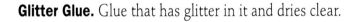

Heat Gun. Used to heat embossing powder and embossing ink to create a shiny, raised image.

Layering. Stamping a number of different images on top of each other.

Masking. Covering an image you've stamped with a piece of paper to keep it from being ruined when you stamp around it or over it.

Pigment Ink Pad. A slow drying ink pad used for embossing.

Pop-Up Card. A card that has pop-out flaps for attaching stamped cut-outs for a 3-D look.

Positioner. A T-Square type object that is used along with see-thru paper to align your stamp, cover mistakes and make straight borders.

Pretty Punches. Hole punches that are pre-cut shapes such as hearts or bears etc.. They can be used as accents or confetti.

Rainbow Stamp Pads. A multi-colored stamp pad.

Sponging. Applying ink to your card with a sponge to give an *airbrushed* look.

Stamp Pad. A pad with colored ink for rubber stamping.

Trinkets. Doilies, rhinestones, lace, metal charms, confetti, mini bows, etc. that can be added to your stamped designs.

Wavy Scissors. Scissors that cut in a wave instead of a straight line.

X-Acto® Knife. A knife with replaceable, sharp thin blades for cutting slits and intricate details.